Contents

Some families live together.

In my house, there's my mum, dad, sister, brother and me.

My dad works in a different country. I talk to him on the computer.

Some families live apart.

What is your family like?

Some children live with two parents. Lots of children live with a mum and a dad.

Some children have two mums, while some children have two dads.

Some children live with just one parent.

This can be just their mum, or just their dad.

Sometimes, mums and dads can't live together. They split up or they may get divorced. One of them may move away and live somewhere else.

When my mum and dad split up, my dad went to live in the next town.

Some children share their time between their mum and dad. The parent who has moved away is still part of their family.

If your parents split up, your mum or dad might find another partner and get married. Their new partner becomes your step-dad or step-mum.

Your step-mum or step-dad might have their own children. Then, you all become part of the same family.

This can feel strange at first.
You might feel shy or upset.

But when you get to know each other,
it can be fun to have more people to
talk to and spend time with.

Some children live separately from their grandparents, uncles, aunties and cousins. They may live close to each other or further away.

Sometimes the whole family lives together in the same place.

Our house is really busy and noisy. But there's always someone to talk to if you feel fed up.

There are all kinds of ways
of making a family.

On the day I was
adopted, we have a
cake to celebrate.

Some children are adopted. This means that they
cannot live with their birth family. A new family is
chosen for them. This is their forever family.

Some children are adopted when they are babies. Some children are adopted when they are older.

My mum and dad adopted me first. Then they adopted my brother.

Some children go to live with a foster family. They may stay for a few weeks or a few years. Afterwards, they may go back to their birth family or they may be adopted.

The foster family may have other children staying with them. They may have their own children living with them, as well.

Families can be very big. Some children have lots of brothers ... or lots of sisters ... or lots of sisters and brothers.

Some families are very small. A family may have only two people in it but it is still a family.

Some children are only children. They don't have any brothers or sisters.

All families fall out sometimes.

Sometimes different people have different feelings about things.

But these feelings can be quick to change.

But being part of a happy family also means feeling safe, loved and looked after.

It means feeling happy to come home.

Everyday life in a family can be very busy, especially at breakfast time.

Some parents go out to work. They rush about getting ready, getting the children to school and getting to work on time.

Most children go to school but some are too young. They may go to a nursery, grandparents or a childminder. They may stay at home with their mum or dad.

After school, some children go to an after-school club or to a childminder until their parents come home from work.

Being part of a family can be lots of fun.

Some families go on holiday. They might dig in the sand. They might fly on a plane. They might visit a theme park. They might just stay at home and snuggle up in front of the TV.

Some families love to celebrate special days. These might be birthdays, weddings or festivals, such as Christmas, Baisakhi, Eid, Diwali or Hanukkah.

Often, these are times for all the family to get together, even if they live far apart.

Who is in your family - mums, dads, aunts, uncles, cousins, grandparents? But families are much more that these.

My mum's best friend is like my auntie.

We go on holiday with our neighbours.

Good friends and neighbours can be very important members of your family. You feel like a part of their family, in turn.

Some people have pet cats, pet dogs, pet rabbits and even pet stick insects. Their pets count as part of their family.

Families can also change over time.

Sometimes, new members are added to a family
and it gets bigger. This happens when a new baby
is born, or someone gets married.

Sometimes, a member of the family dies and the family gets smaller. There are all kinds of families. They can be big, small, loud or quiet. They may live together, or far away. They fall out, and make up.

Every family is different. So, what is your family like?

Notes for teachers, parents and carers

This book introduces children to the topic of families, and the many ways in which families may be put together and change over time. The book aims to show children that there is no such thing as a 'normal' family. Families come in all shapes and sizes – single-parent, single-sex, blended families, foster and adoptive families, and so on.

You may find it useful to start a discussion about different kinds of families by talking about your child's own family, and the families of their friends. You could then encourage them to find out more about their family, and put the information together as a family tree, with small artwork portraits or photographs.

Here are some additional activities that support and expand on the scenarios shown in the book.

Coping with changes

Changes in family life, such as divorce or remarriage, can be extremely unsettling and confusing experiences for children. It is important to allow children time to talk about how they are feeling and ask any questions. Be honest about what is happening, though what you say will inevitably depend on the age of the child. Acknowledge that they may be feeling frightened or sad, but stress that they are still loved, and that both of their parents will continue to look after them.

Showing support in adoption

Some families are formed by adoption, and this can raise many questions both from the adopted child, and from their classmates and other friends. An adopted child might feel upset if their friends tease them because they are adopted. It is important to talk to them about adoption, and to suggest ways for them to handle any negative comments. It might also be worth suggesting to school that they talk to the pupils about adoption, and the importance of inclusion, more generally, without singling any individual child out.

Useful websites

https://www.familylives.org.uk/
Support for anyone who plays an active role in raising children, aiming to help them achieve the best possible relationship.

https://www.relate.org.uk/
Helping people of all ages and backgrounds to strengthen their relationships.

https://www.childline.org.uk/
Advice and support for young people under the age of 19 with any issue they may be going through.

https://www.nspcc.org.uk/
Offering help and support to children and giving them the understanding they need to stay safe from abuse.

https://www.adoptionuk.org/
Support for all those parenting or supporting children who cannot live with their birth parents.

http://www.pac-uk.org/
Information, advice and support for all those affected by adoption.

Useful words

adopted   part of a family different from a birth family.

divorce   when two people end their marriage.

foster family   a family in which children are cared for by people who are not their parents.

homesick   the feeling of missing home very much when you are away from it.

only child   a child in a family who does not have brothers or sisters.

partner   each person in a couple.

Index